INFORMATION

BELONGS TO	
Registration Details	
Address:	

Phone No.		Fax No.	
Email		Emergency No.	
Website			
Work Number			

Continued From Log Book:		Continued To Log Book:	
Date Log Started:		Date Log Ended:	

NOTES

_____

_____

_____

_____

_____

_____

www.signatureplannerjournals.com
www.signatureplannerjournals.co.uk

INDEX PAGE

Item Number	GUN	Page Number
1		
2		
3		
4		
5		
6		
7		
8		
9		
10		
11		
12		
13		
14		
15		
16		
17		
18		
19		
20		
21		
22		
23		
24		
25		

INDEX PAGE

Item Number	GUN	Page Number
26		
27		
28		
29		
30		
31		
32		
33		
34		
35		
36		
37		
38		
39		
40		
41		
42		
43		
44		
45		
46		
47		
48		
49		
50		

INSURANCE DETAILS

COMPANY	
POLICY NUMBER	
START DATE	END DATE
PRICE	
COVERAGE TYPE	
CONTACT NUMBER	
EMAIL	
FAX	
WEBSITE	
NOTES	

COMPANY	
POLICY NUMBER	
START DATE	END DATE
PRICE	
COVERAGE TYPE	
CONTACT NUMBER	
EMAIL	
FAX	
WEBSITE	
NOTES	

COMPANY	
POLICY NUMBER	
START DATE	END DATE
PRICE	
COVERAGE TYPE	
CONTACT NUMBER	
EMAIL	
FAX	
WEBSITE	
NOTES	

INSURANCE DETAILS

COMPANY	
POLICY NUMBER	
START DATE	END DATE
PRICE	
COVERAGE TYPE	
CONTACT NUMBER	
EMAIL	
FAX	
WEBSITE	
NOTES	

COMPANY	
POLICY NUMBER	
START DATE	END DATE
PRICE	
COVERAGE TYPE	
CONTACT NUMBER	
EMAIL	
FAX	
WEBSITE	
NOTES	

COMPANY	
POLICY NUMBER	
START DATE	END DATE
PRICE	
COVERAGE TYPE	
CONTACT NUMBER	
EMAIL	
FAX	
WEBSITE	
NOTES	

FIREARM DETAILS

GUN #

FIREARM TYPE	Handgun	Shotgun	Rifle	Pistol	
	Air gun	Other			

Serial Number				
Manufacturer		Model/ Type		
Caliber		Capacity		
Weight		Identifiers		
Barrel Length		Barrel Type	Standard	Target
			Bull	Other

Action:	Single Shot	Semi-Auto	Bolt	Single Action	
	Revolver	Full- Auto	Lever	Double Action	
	Pump	Muzzle Loader	Other		

Description	
Alterations	
Repairs	

✎ **NOTES**

ACQUISITION & DISPOSITION INFORMATION

PURCHASED FROM	
ADDRESS	
CONTACT NUMBER	

DATE		PRICE PAID	
ID Number		D.O.B	
CONDITION			
COMMENTS			

DISPOSITION

TRANSFER/SOLD TO	
ADDRESS	
CONTACT NUMBER	

DATE		PRICE SOLD	
ID Number		D.O.B	
LOST/ STOLEN		CONDITION	
DETAILS			

IN THE EVENT OF MY DEMISE I WANT THIS FIREARM TO GO TO:	

NOTES

FIREARM DETAILS

GUN #	

FIREARM TYPE	Handgun		Shotgun		Rifle		Pistol		
	Air gun		Other						

Serial Number				
Manufacturer		Model/ Type		
Caliber		Capacity		
Weight		Identifiers		
Barrel Length		Barrel Type	Standard	Target	
			Bull	Other	

Action:	Single Shot		Semi-Auto		Bolt		Single Action	
	Revolver		Full- Auto		Lever		Double Action	
	Pump		Muzzle Loader		Other			

Description	
Alterations	
Repairs	

✎ NOTES

ACQUISITION & DISPOSITION INFORMATION

PURCHASED FROM	
ADDRESS	
CONTACT NUMBER	
DATE	PRICE PAID
ID Number	D.O.B
CONDITION	
COMMENTS	

DISPOSITION

TRANSFER/SOLD TO	
ADDRESS	
CONTACT NUMBER	
DATE	PRICE SOLD
ID Number	D.O.B
LOST/ STOLEN	CONDITION
DETAILS	

IN THE EVENT OF MY DEMISE I WANT THIS FIREARM TO GO TO:

NOTES

FIREARM DETAILS

GUN #	

FIREARM TYPE	Handgun	Shotgun		Rifle		Pistol	
	Air gun	Other					

Serial Number							
Manufacturer		Model/ Type					
Caliber		Capacity					
Weight		Identifiers					
Barrel Length		Barrel Type		Standard		Target	
				Bull		Other	
Action:	Single Shot	Semi-Auto	Bolt	Single Action	
	Revolver	Full- Auto	Lever	Double Action	
	Pump	Muzzle Loader	Other		
Description	
Alterations	
Repairs	

✎ **NOTES**

ACQUISITION & DISPOSITION INFORMATION

PURCHASED FROM	
ADDRESS	
CONTACT NUMBER	
DATE	PRICE PAID
ID Number	D.O.B
CONDITION	
COMMENTS	

DISPOSITION

TRANSFER/SOLD TO	
ADDRESS	
CONTACT NUMBER	
DATE	PRICE SOLD
ID Number	D.O.B
LOST/ STOLEN	CONDITION
DETAILS	

IN THE EVENT OF MY DEMISE I WANT THIS FIREARM TO GO TO:

NOTES

FIREARM DETAILS

GUN #

FIREARM TYPE	Handgun		Shotgun		Rifle		Pistol	
	Air gun		Other					

Serial Number								
Manufacturer		Model/ Type						
Caliber		Capacity						
Weight		Identifiers						
Barrel Length		Barrel Type			Standard		Target	
					Bull		Other	
Action:	Single Shot		Semi-Auto		Bolt		Single Action	
	Revolver		Full- Auto		Lever		Double Action	
	Pump		Muzzle Loader		Other			
Description								
Alterations								
Repairs								

✎ **NOTES**

ACQUISITION & DISPOSITION INFORMATION

PURCHASED FROM	
ADDRESS	
CONTACT NUMBER	
DATE	PRICE PAID
ID Number	D.O.B
CONDITION	
COMMENTS	

DISPOSITION

TRANSFER/SOLD TO	
ADDRESS	
CONTACT NUMBER	
DATE	PRICE SOLD
ID Number	D.O.B
LOST/ STOLEN	CONDITION
DETAILS	

IN THE EVENT OF MY DEMISE I WANT THIS FIREARM TO GO TO:	

NOTES

FIREARM DETAILS

GUN #	

FIREARM TYPE	Handgun		Shotgun		Rifle		Pistol	
	Air gun		Other					

Serial Number						
Manufacturer		**Model/ Type**				
Caliber		**Capacity**				
Weight		**Identifiers**				
Barrel Length		**Barrel Type**	Standard		Target	
			Bull		Other	
Action:	Single Shot	Semi-Auto	Bolt	Single Action	
	Revolver	Full- Auto	Lever	Double Action	
	Pump	Muzzle Loader	Other		
Description						
Alterations						
Repairs						

✎ **NOTES**

9

ACQUISITION & DISPOSITION INFORMATION

PURCHASED FROM			
ADDRESS			
CONTACT NUMBER			
DATE		PRICE PAID	
ID Number		D.O.B	
CONDITION			
COMMENTS			

DISPOSITION

TRANSFER/SOLD TO			
ADDRESS			
CONTACT NUMBER			
DATE		PRICE SOLD	
ID Number		D.O.B	
LOST/ STOLEN		CONDITION	
DETAILS			

IN THE EVENT OF MY DEMISE I WANT THIS FIREARM TO GO TO:

NOTES

FIREARM DETAILS

GUN #

FIREARM TYPE	Handgun		Shotgun		Rifle		Pistol	
	Air gun		Other					

Serial Number								
Manufacturer			Model/ Type					
Caliber			Capacity					
Weight			Identifiers					
Barrel Length			Barrel Type		Standard		Target	
					Bull		Other	
Action:	Single Shot		Semi-Auto		Bolt		Single Action	
	Revolver		Full- Auto		Lever		Double Action	
	Pump		Muzzle Loader		Other			
Description								
Alterations								
Repairs								

✎ **NOTES**

ACQUISITION & DISPOSITION INFORMATION

PURCHASED FROM	
ADDRESS	
CONTACT NUMBER	
DATE	PRICE PAID
ID Number	D.O.B
CONDITION	
COMMENTS	

DISPOSITION

TRANSFER/SOLD TO	
ADDRESS	
CONTACT NUMBER	
DATE	PRICE SOLD
ID Number	D.O.B
LOST/ STOLEN	CONDITION
DETAILS	

IN THE EVENT OF MY DEMISE I WANT THIS FIREARM TO GO TO:	

NOTES

FIREARM DETAILS

GUN #	

FIREARM TYPE	Handgun	Shotgun		Rifle		Pistol	
	Air gun	Other					

Serial Number				
Manufacturer		Model/ Type		
Caliber		Capacity		
Weight		Identifiers		

Barrel Length		Barrel Type	Standard	Target	
			Bull	Other	

Action:	Single Shot	Semi-Auto	Bolt	Single Action	
	Revolver	Full- Auto	Lever	Double Action	
	Pump	Muzzle Loader	Other		

Description	
Alterations	
Repairs	

✎ NOTES

ACQUISITION & DISPOSITION INFORMATION

PURCHASED FROM	
ADDRESS	
CONTACT NUMBER	
DATE	PRICE PAID	
ID Number	D.O.B	
CONDITION	
COMMENTS	

DISPOSITION

TRANSFER/SOLD TO	
ADDRESS	
CONTACT NUMBER	
DATE	PRICE SOLD	
ID Number	D.O.B	
LOST/ STOLEN	CONDITION	
DETAILS	

IN THE EVENT OF MY DEMISE I WANT THIS FIREARM TO GO TO:

NOTES

FIREARM DETAILS

GUN #

FIREARM TYPE	Handgun		Shotgun		Rifle		Pistol	
	Air gun		Other					

Serial Number										
Manufacturer		Model/ Type								
Caliber		Capacity								
Weight		Identifiers								
Barrel Length		Barrel Type		Standard		Target				
				Bull		Other				
Action:	Single Shot		Semi-Auto		Bolt		Single Action			
	Revolver		Full- Auto		Lever		Double Action			
	Pump		Muzzle Loader		Other					
Description										
Alterations										
Repairs										
✎ NOTES										

ACQUISITION & DISPOSITION INFORMATION

PURCHASED FROM	
ADDRESS	
CONTACT NUMBER	
DATE	
ID Number	
CONDITION	
COMMENTS	

	PRICE PAID	
	D.O.B	

DISPOSITION

TRANSFER/SOLD TO	
ADDRESS	
CONTACT NUMBER	
DATE	
ID Number	
LOST/ STOLEN	
DETAILS	

	PRICE SOLD	
	D.O.B	
	CONDITION	

IN THE EVENT OF MY DEMISE I WANT THIS FIREARM TO GO TO:

NOTES

_____

_____

_____

_____

_____

_____

_____

FIREARM DETAILS

GUN #

FIREARM TYPE	Handgun		Shotgun		Rifle		Pistol	
	Air gun		Other					

Serial Number							
Manufacturer		Model/ Type					
Caliber		Capacity					
Weight		Identifiers					
Barrel Length		Barrel Type		Standard		Target	
				Bull		Other	
Action:	Single Shot	Semi-Auto	Bolt	Single Action	
	Revolver	Full- Auto	Lever	Double Action	
	Pump	Muzzle Loader	Other		
Description							
Alterations							
Repairs							

✎ **NOTES**

17

ACQUISITION & DISPOSITION INFORMATION

PURCHASED FROM	
ADDRESS	
CONTACT NUMBER	
DATE	PRICE PAID
ID Number	D.O.B
CONDITION	
COMMENTS	

DISPOSITION

TRANSFER/SOLD TO	
ADDRESS	
CONTACT NUMBER	
DATE	PRICE SOLD
ID Number	D.O.B
LOST/ STOLEN	CONDITION
DETAILS	

IN THE EVENT OF MY DEMISE I WANT THIS FIREARM TO GO TO:	

NOTES

FIREARM DETAILS

GUN #

FIREARM TYPE	Handgun		Shotgun		Rifle		Pistol	
	Air gun		Other					

Serial Number								
Manufacturer			Model/ Type					
Caliber			Capacity					
Weight			Identifiers					
Barrel Length			Barrel Type		Standard		Target	
					Bull		Other	
Action:	Single Shot		Semi-Auto		Bolt		Single Action	
	Revolver		Full- Auto		Lever		Double Action	
	Pump		Muzzle Loader		Other			
Description								
Alterations								
Repairs								

✎ **NOTES**

ACQUISITION & DISPOSITION INFORMATION

PURCHASED FROM	
ADDRESS	
CONTACT NUMBER	
DATE	PRICE PAID
ID Number	D.O.B
CONDITION	
COMMENTS	

DISPOSITION

TRANSFER/SOLD TO	
ADDRESS	
CONTACT NUMBER	
DATE	PRICE SOLD
ID Number	D.O.B
LOST/ STOLEN	CONDITION
DETAILS	

IN THE EVENT OF MY DEMISE I WANT THIS FIREARM TO GO TO:	

NOTES

FIREARM DETAILS

GUN #	

FIREARM TYPE	Handgun		Shotgun		Rifle		Pistol	
	Air gun		Other					

Serial Number				
Manufacturer		Model/ Type		
Caliber		Capacity		
Weight		Identifiers		

Barrel Length		Barrel Type	Standard		Target	
			Bull		Other	

Action:	Single Shot		Semi-Auto		Bolt		Single Action	
	Revolver		Full- Auto		Lever		Double Action	
	Pump		Muzzle Loader		Other			

Description	
Alterations	
Repairs	

✎ **NOTES**

ACQUISITION & DISPOSITION INFORMATION

PURCHASED FROM	
ADDRESS	
CONTACT NUMBER	
DATE	PRICE PAID	
ID Number	D.O.B	
CONDITION	
COMMENTS	

DISPOSITION

TRANSFER/SOLD TO	
ADDRESS	
CONTACT NUMBER	
DATE	PRICE SOLD	
ID Number	D.O.B	
LOST/ STOLEN	CONDITION	
DETAILS	

IN THE EVENT OF MY DEMISE I WANT THIS FIREARM TO GO TO:

NOTES

FIREARM DETAILS

GUN

FIREARM TYPE	Handgun		Shotgun		Rifle		Pistol	
	Air gun		Other					

Serial Number				
Manufacturer		Model/ Type		
Caliber		Capacity		
Weight		Identifiers		
Barrel Length		Barrel Type	Standard / Bull	Target / Other

Action:	Single Shot	Semi-Auto	Bolt	Single Action
	Revolver	Full- Auto	Lever	Double Action
	Pump	Muzzle Loader	Other	

Description	
Alterations	
Repairs	

✎ **NOTES**

ACQUISITION & DISPOSITION INFORMATION

PURCHASED FROM	
ADDRESS	
CONTACT NUMBER	
DATE	PRICE PAID	
ID Number	D.O.B	
CONDITION	
COMMENTS	

DISPOSITION

TRANSFER/SOLD TO	
ADDRESS	
CONTACT NUMBER	
DATE	PRICE SOLD	
ID Number	D.O.B	
LOST/ STOLEN	CONDITION	
DETAILS	

IN THE EVENT OF MY DEMISE I WANT THIS FIREARM TO GO TO:	

NOTES

FIREARM DETAILS

GUN #

FIREARM TYPE	Handgun		Shotgun		Rifle		Pistol	
	Air gun		Other					

Serial Number							
Manufacturer			Model/ Type				
Caliber			Capacity				
Weight			Identifiers				
Barrel Length			Barrel Type		Standard		Target	
					Bull		Other	

Action:	Single Shot		Semi-Auto		Bolt		Single Action	
	Revolver		Full- Auto		Lever		Double Action	
	Pump		Muzzle Loader		Other			

Description	
Alterations	
Repairs	

✎ NOTES

ACQUISITION & DISPOSITION INFORMATION

PURCHASED FROM	
ADDRESS	
CONTACT NUMBER	
DATE	PRICE PAID
ID Number	D.O.B
CONDITION	
COMMENTS	

DISPOSITION

TRANSFER/SOLD TO	
ADDRESS	
CONTACT NUMBER	
DATE	PRICE SOLD
ID Number	D.O.B
LOST/ STOLEN	CONDITION
DETAILS	

IN THE EVENT OF MY DEMISE I WANT THIS FIREARM TO GO TO:	

NOTES

_____
_____
_____
_____
_____
_____
_____

FIREARM DETAILS

GUN #

FIREARM TYPE	Handgun		Shotgun		Rifle		Pistol	
	Air gun		Other					

Serial Number				
Manufacturer		Model/ Type		
Caliber		Capacity		
Weight		Identifiers		
Barrel Length		Barrel Type	Standard / Bull	Target / Other

Action:	Single Shot	Semi-Auto	Bolt	Single Action
	Revolver	Full- Auto	Lever	Double Action
	Pump	Muzzle Loader	Other	

Description	
Alterations	
Repairs	

✎ NOTES

27

ACQUISITION & DISPOSITION INFORMATION

PURCHASED FROM	
ADDRESS	
CONTACT NUMBER	
DATE	PRICE PAID	
ID Number	D.O.B	
CONDITION	
COMMENTS	

DISPOSITION

TRANSFER/SOLD TO	
ADDRESS	
CONTACT NUMBER	
DATE	PRICE SOLD	
ID Number	D.O.B	
LOST/ STOLEN	CONDITION	
DETAILS	

IN THE EVENT OF MY DEMISE I WANT THIS FIREARM TO GO TO:

NOTES

FIREARM DETAILS

GUN #

FIREARM TYPE	Handgun		Shotgun		Rifle		Pistol	
	Air gun		Other					

Serial Number				
Manufacturer		Model/ Type		
Caliber		Capacity		
Weight		Identifiers		

Barrel Length		Barrel Type	Standard		Target	
			Bull		Other	

Action:	Single Shot		Semi-Auto		Bolt		Single Action	
	Revolver		Full- Auto		Lever		Double Action	
	Pump		Muzzle Loader		Other			

Description	
Alterations	
Repairs	

✎ **NOTES**

ACQUISITION & DISPOSITION INFORMATION

PURCHASED FROM	
ADDRESS	
CONTACT NUMBER	
DATE	PRICE PAID
ID Number	D.O.B
CONDITION	
COMMENTS	

DISPOSITION

TRANSFER/SOLD TO	
ADDRESS	
CONTACT NUMBER	
DATE	PRICE SOLD
ID Number	D.O.B
LOST/ STOLEN	CONDITION
DETAILS	

IN THE EVENT OF MY DEMISE I WANT THIS FIREARM TO GO TO:	

NOTES

FIREARM DETAILS

GUN #

FIREARM TYPE	Handgun		Shotgun		Rifle		Pistol	
	Air gun		Other					

Serial Number						
Manufacturer		Model/ Type				
Caliber		Capacity				
Weight		Identifiers				
Barrel Length		Barrel Type		Standard		Target	
				Bull		Other	
Action:	Single Shot		Semi-Auto		Bolt		Single Action	
	Revolver		Full- Auto		Lever		Double Action	
	Pump		Muzzle Loader		Other			
Description						
Alterations						
Repairs						

✎ **NOTES**

31

ACQUISITION & DISPOSITION INFORMATION

PURCHASED FROM	
ADDRESS	
CONTACT NUMBER	
DATE	PRICE PAID
ID Number	D.O.B
CONDITION	
COMMENTS	

DISPOSITION

TRANSFER/SOLD TO	
ADDRESS	
CONTACT NUMBER	
DATE	PRICE SOLD
ID Number	D.O.B
LOST/ STOLEN	CONDITION
DETAILS	

IN THE EVENT OF MY DEMISE I WANT THIS FIREARM TO GO TO:	

NOTES

FIREARM DETAILS

GUN #

FIREARM TYPE	Handgun		Shotgun		Rifle		Pistol	
	Air gun		Other					

Serial Number								
Manufacturer		Model/ Type						
Caliber		Capacity						
Weight		Identifiers						
Barrel Length		Barrel Type		Standard		Target		
				Bull		Other		
Action:	Single Shot		Semi-Auto		Bolt		Single Action	
	Revolver		Full- Auto		Lever		Double Action	
	Pump		Muzzle Loader		Other			
Description								
Alterations								
Repairs								
✏ NOTES								

33

ACQUISITION & DISPOSITION INFORMATION

PURCHASED FROM	
ADDRESS	
CONTACT NUMBER	
DATE		PRICE PAID	
ID Number		D.O.B	
CONDITION	
COMMENTS	

DISPOSITION

TRANSFER/SOLD TO	
ADDRESS	
CONTACT NUMBER	
DATE		PRICE SOLD	
ID Number		D.O.B	
LOST/ STOLEN		CONDITION	
DETAILS	

IN THE EVENT OF MY DEMISE I WANT THIS FIREARM TO GO TO:

NOTES

FIREARM DETAILS

GUN #	

FIREARM TYPE	Handgun		Shotgun		Rifle		Pistol	
	Air gun		Other					

Serial Number				
Manufacturer		Model/ Type		
Caliber		Capacity		
Weight		Identifiers		

Barrel Length		Barrel Type	Standard		Target	
			Bull		Other	

Action:	Single Shot		Semi-Auto		Bolt		Single Action	
	Revolver		Full- Auto		Lever		Double Action	
	Pump		Muzzle Loader		Other			

Description	
Alterations	
Repairs	

✎ **NOTES**

35

ACQUISITION & DISPOSITION INFORMATION

PURCHASED FROM	
ADDRESS	
CONTACT NUMBER	
DATE	PRICE PAID
ID Number	D.O.B
CONDITION	
COMMENTS	

DISPOSITION

TRANSFER/SOLD TO	
ADDRESS	
CONTACT NUMBER	
DATE	PRICE SOLD
ID Number	D.O.B
LOST/ STOLEN	CONDITION
DETAILS	

IN THE EVENT OF MY DEMISE I WANT THIS FIREARM TO GO TO:	

NOTES

FIREARM DETAILS

GUN #	

FIREARM TYPE	Handgun		Shotgun		Rifle		Pistol	
	Air gun		Other					

Serial Number				
Manufacturer		Model/ Type		
Caliber		Capacity		
Weight		Identifiers		

Barrel Length			Barrel Type	Standard		Target	
				Bull		Other	

Action:	Single Shot		Semi-Auto		Bolt		Single Action	
	Revolver		Full- Auto		Lever		Double Action	
	Pump		Muzzle Loader		Other			

Description	
Alterations	
Repairs	

✏ **NOTES**

ACQUISITION & DISPOSITION INFORMATION

PURCHASED FROM	
ADDRESS	
CONTACT NUMBER	
DATE	
ID Number	
CONDITION	
COMMENTS	

		PRICE PAID	
		D.O.B	

DISPOSITION

TRANSFER/SOLD TO	
ADDRESS	
CONTACT NUMBER	
DATE	
ID Number	
LOST/ STOLEN	
DETAILS	

		PRICE SOLD	
		D.O.B	
		CONDITION	

IN THE EVENT OF MY DEMISE I WANT THIS FIREARM TO GO TO:	

NOTES

FIREARM DETAILS

GUN #

FIREARM TYPE	Handgun		Shotgun		Rifle		Pistol	
	Air gun		Other					

Serial Number			
Manufacturer		Model/ Type	
Caliber		Capacity	
Weight		Identifiers	

Barrel Length		Barrel Type	Standard		Target	
			Bull		Other	

Action:	Single Shot		Semi-Auto		Bolt		Single Action	
	Revolver		Full- Auto		Lever		Double Action	
	Pump		Muzzle Loader		Other			

Description	
Alterations	
Repairs	

✎ **NOTES**

ACQUISITION & DISPOSITION INFORMATION

PURCHASED FROM	
ADDRESS	
CONTACT NUMBER	
DATE	PRICE PAID	
ID Number	D.O.B	
CONDITION	
COMMENTS	

DISPOSITION

TRANSFER/SOLD TO	
ADDRESS	
CONTACT NUMBER	
DATE	PRICE SOLD	
ID Number	D.O.B	
LOST/ STOLEN	CONDITION	
DETAILS	

IN THE EVENT OF MY DEMISE I WANT THIS FIREARM TO GO TO:

NOTES

FIREARM DETAILS

GUN #

FIREARM TYPE	Handgun		Shotgun		Rifle		Pistol	
	Air gun		Other					

Serial Number									
Manufacturer			Model/ Type						
Caliber			Capacity						
Weight			Identifiers						
Barrel Length			Barrel Type		Standard		Target		
					Bull		Other		
Action:	Single Shot		Semi-Auto		Bolt		Single Action		
	Revolver		Full- Auto		Lever		Double Action		
	Pump		Muzzle Loader		Other				
Description									
Alterations									
Repairs									

✎ NOTES

41

ACQUISITION & DISPOSITION INFORMATION

PURCHASED FROM	
ADDRESS	
CONTACT NUMBER	
DATE	PRICE PAID
ID Number	D.O.B
CONDITION	
COMMENTS	

DISPOSITION

TRANSFER/SOLD TO	
ADDRESS	
CONTACT NUMBER	
DATE	PRICE SOLD
ID Number	D.O.B
LOST/ STOLEN	CONDITION
DETAILS	

IN THE EVENT OF MY DEMISE I WANT THIS FIREARM TO GO TO:	

NOTES

FIREARM DETAILS

GUN #

FIREARM TYPE	Handgun		Shotgun		Rifle		Pistol	
	Air gun		Other					

Serial Number							
Manufacturer		Model/ Type					
Caliber		Capacity					
Weight		Identifiers					
Barrel Length		Barrel Type		Standard		Target	
				Bull		Other	
Action:	Single Shot	Semi-Auto	Bolt	Single Action	
	Revolver	Full- Auto	Lever	Double Action	
	Pump	Muzzle Loader	Other		
Description							
Alterations							
Repairs							

✎ **NOTES**

43

ACQUISITION & DISPOSITION INFORMATION

PURCHASED FROM	
ADDRESS	
CONTACT NUMBER	
DATE	PRICE PAID
ID Number	D.O.B
CONDITION	
COMMENTS	

DISPOSITION

TRANSFER/SOLD TO	
ADDRESS	
CONTACT NUMBER	
DATE	PRICE SOLD
ID Number	D.O.B
LOST/ STOLEN	CONDITION
DETAILS	

IN THE EVENT OF MY DEMISE I WANT THIS FIREARM TO GO TO:	

NOTES

_____

_____

_____

_____

_____

_____

_____

FIREARM DETAILS

GUN #

FIREARM TYPE	Handgun		Shotgun		Rifle		Pistol	
	Air gun		Other					

Serial Number							
Manufacturer		Model/ Type					
Caliber		Capacity					
Weight		Identifiers					
Barrel Length		Barrel Type		Standard		Target	
				Bull		Other	
Action:	Single Shot	Semi-Auto	Bolt	Single Action	
	Revolver	Full- Auto	Lever	Double Action	
	Pump	Muzzle Loader	Other		
Description							
Alterations							
Repairs							

✎ **NOTES**

ACQUISITION & DISPOSITION INFORMATION

PURCHASED FROM	
ADDRESS	
CONTACT NUMBER	
DATE	PRICE PAID
ID Number	D.O.B
CONDITION	
COMMENTS	

DISPOSITION

TRANSFER/SOLD TO	
ADDRESS	
CONTACT NUMBER	
DATE	PRICE SOLD
ID Number	D.O.B
LOST/ STOLEN	CONDITION
DETAILS	

IN THE EVENT OF MY DEMISE I WANT THIS FIREARM TO GO TO:	

NOTES

FIREARM DETAILS

GUN #	

FIREARM TYPE	Handgun		Shotgun		Rifle		Pistol	
	Air gun		Other					

Serial Number						
Manufacturer			Model/ Type			
Caliber			Capacity			
Weight			Identifiers			
Barrel Length			Barrel Type		Standard	Target
					Bull	Other

Action:	Single Shot		Semi-Auto		Bolt		Single Action	
	Revolver		Full- Auto		Lever		Double Action	
	Pump		Muzzle Loader		Other			

Description	
Alterations	
Repairs	

✎ NOTES

ACQUISITION & DISPOSITION INFORMATION

PURCHASED FROM	
ADDRESS	
CONTACT NUMBER	
DATE	PRICE PAID
ID Number	D.O.B
CONDITION	
COMMENTS	

DISPOSITION

TRANSFER/SOLD TO	
ADDRESS	
CONTACT NUMBER	
DATE	PRICE SOLD
ID Number	D.O.B
LOST/ STOLEN	CONDITION
DETAILS	

IN THE EVENT OF MY DEMISE I WANT THIS FIREARM TO GO TO:	

NOTES

FIREARM DETAILS

GUN #

FIREARM TYPE	Handgun		Shotgun		Rifle		Pistol	
	Air gun		Other					

Serial Number							
Manufacturer		Model/ Type					
Caliber		Capacity					
Weight		Identifiers					
Barrel Length		Barrel Type		Standard		Target	
				Bull		Other	
Action:	Single Shot		Semi-Auto		Bolt		Single Action	
	Revolver		Full- Auto		Lever		Double Action	
	Pump		Muzzle Loader		Other			
Description							
Alterations							
Repairs							

✎ **NOTES**

ACQUISITION & DISPOSITION INFORMATION

PURCHASED FROM	
ADDRESS	
CONTACT NUMBER	
DATE	PRICE PAID
ID Number	D.O.B
CONDITION	
COMMENTS	

DISPOSITION

TRANSFER/SOLD TO	
ADDRESS	
CONTACT NUMBER	
DATE	PRICE SOLD
ID Number	D.O.B
LOST/ STOLEN	CONDITION
DETAILS	

IN THE EVENT OF MY DEMISE I WANT THIS FIREARM TO GO TO:	

NOTES

FIREARM DETAILS

GUN #	

FIREARM TYPE	Handgun		Shotgun		Rifle		Pistol	
	Air gun		Other					

Serial Number							
Manufacturer		Model/ Type					
Caliber		Capacity					
Weight		Identifiers					
Barrel Length		Barrel Type		Standard		Target	
				Bull		Other	

Action:	Single Shot		Semi-Auto		Bolt		Single Action	
	Revolver		Full- Auto		Lever		Double Action	
	Pump		Muzzle Loader		Other			

Description	
Alterations	
Repairs	

✎ **NOTES**

ACQUISITION & DISPOSITION INFORMATION

PURCHASED FROM	
ADDRESS	
CONTACT NUMBER	
DATE	PRICE PAID
ID Number	D.O.B
CONDITION	
COMMENTS	

DISPOSITION

TRANSFER/SOLD TO	
ADDRESS	
CONTACT NUMBER	
DATE	PRICE SOLD
ID Number	D.O.B
LOST/ STOLEN	CONDITION
DETAILS	

IN THE EVENT OF MY DEMISE I WANT THIS FIREARM TO GO TO:

NOTES

FIREARM DETAILS

GUN #	

FIREARM TYPE	Handgun		Shotgun		Rifle		Pistol	
	Air gun		Other					

Serial Number							
Manufacturer		Model/ Type					
Caliber		Capacity					
Weight		Identifiers					
Barrel Length		Barrel Type		Standard		Target	
				Bull		Other	

Action:	Single Shot		Semi-Auto		Bolt		Single Action	
	Revolver		Full- Auto		Lever		Double Action	
	Pump		Muzzle Loader		Other			

Description	
Alterations	
Repairs	

✎ **NOTES**

ACQUISITION & DISPOSITION INFORMATION

PURCHASED FROM	
ADDRESS	
CONTACT NUMBER	
DATE	PRICE PAID
ID Number	D.O.B
CONDITION	
COMMENTS	

DISPOSITION

TRANSFER/SOLD TO	
ADDRESS	
CONTACT NUMBER	
DATE	PRICE SOLD
ID Number	D.O.B
LOST/ STOLEN	CONDITION
DETAILS	

IN THE EVENT OF MY DEMISE I WANT THIS FIREARM TO GO TO:	

NOTES

FIREARM DETAILS

GUN #

FIREARM TYPE	Handgun		Shotgun			Rifle		Pistol	
	Air gun		Other						

Serial Number										
Manufacturer			Model/ Type							
Caliber			Capacity							
Weight			Identifiers							
Barrel Length			Barrel Type			Standard		Target		
						Bull		Other		
Action:	Single Shot		Semi-Auto		Bolt		Single Action			
	Revolver		Full- Auto		Lever		Double Action			
	Pump		Muzzle Loader		Other					
Description										
Alterations										
Repairs										
✎ NOTES										

ACQUISITION & DISPOSITION INFORMATION

PURCHASED FROM	
ADDRESS	
CONTACT NUMBER	
DATE	PRICE PAID
ID Number	D.O.B
CONDITION	
COMMENTS	

DISPOSITION

TRANSFER/SOLD TO	
ADDRESS	
CONTACT NUMBER	
DATE	PRICE SOLD
ID Number	D.O.B
LOST/ STOLEN	CONDITION
DETAILS	

IN THE EVENT OF MY DEMISE I WANT THIS FIREARM TO GO TO:	

NOTES

FIREARM DETAILS

GUN #

FIREARM TYPE	Handgun		Shotgun		Rifle		Pistol	
	Air gun		Other					

Serial Number				
Manufacturer		Model/ Type		
Caliber		Capacity		
Weight		Identifiers		

Barrel Length		Barrel Type	Standard		Target	
			Bull		Other	

Action:	Single Shot		Semi-Auto		Bolt		Single Action	
	Revolver		Full- Auto		Lever		Double Action	
	Pump		Muzzle Loader		Other			

Description	
Alterations	
Repairs	

✎ **NOTES**

ACQUISITION & DISPOSITION INFORMATION

PURCHASED FROM	
ADDRESS	
CONTACT NUMBER	
DATE	PRICE PAID
ID Number	D.O.B
CONDITION	
COMMENTS	

DISPOSITION

TRANSFER/SOLD TO	
ADDRESS	
CONTACT NUMBER	
DATE	PRICE SOLD
ID Number	D.O.B
LOST/ STOLEN	CONDITION
DETAILS	

IN THE EVENT OF MY DEMISE I WANT THIS FIREARM TO GO TO:	

NOTES

FIREARM DETAILS

GUN #	

FIREARM TYPE	Handgun		Shotgun		Rifle		Pistol	
	Air gun		Other					

Serial Number							
Manufacturer		Model/ Type					
Caliber		Capacity					
Weight		Identifiers					
Barrel Length		Barrel Type		Standard		Target	
				Bull		Other	
Action:	Single Shot		Semi-Auto		Bolt		Single Action	
	Revolver		Full- Auto		Lever		Double Action	
	Pump		Muzzle Loader		Other			
Description							
Alterations							
Repairs							

✎ NOTES

ACQUISITION & DISPOSITION INFORMATION

PURCHASED FROM	
ADDRESS	
CONTACT NUMBER	
DATE	PRICE PAID
ID Number	D.O.B
CONDITION	
COMMENTS	

DISPOSITION

TRANSFER/SOLD TO	
ADDRESS	
CONTACT NUMBER	
DATE	PRICE SOLD
ID Number	D.O.B
LOST/ STOLEN	CONDITION
DETAILS	

IN THE EVENT OF MY DEMISE I WANT THIS FIREARM TO GO TO:	

NOTES

FIREARM DETAILS

GUN #

FIREARM TYPE	Handgun		Shotgun		Rifle		Pistol	
	Air gun		Other					

Serial Number				
Manufacturer		Model/ Type		
Caliber		Capacity		
Weight		Identifiers		
Barrel Length		Barrel Type	Standard	Target
			Bull	Other

Action:	Single Shot		Semi-Auto		Bolt		Single Action	
	Revolver		Full- Auto		Lever		Double Action	
	Pump		Muzzle Loader		Other			

Description	
Alterations	
Repairs	
✎ NOTES	

61

ACQUISITION & DISPOSITION INFORMATION

PURCHASED FROM	
ADDRESS	
CONTACT NUMBER	
DATE		PRICE PAID	
ID Number		D.O.B	
CONDITION	
COMMENTS	

DISPOSITION

TRANSFER/SOLD TO	
ADDRESS	
CONTACT NUMBER	
DATE		PRICE SOLD	
ID Number		D.O.B	
LOST/ STOLEN		CONDITION	
DETAILS	

IN THE EVENT OF MY DEMISE I WANT THIS FIREARM TO GO TO:	

NOTES

_____

_____

_____

_____

_____

_____

_____

_____

FIREARM DETAILS

GUN #

FIREARM TYPE	Handgun		Shotgun		Rifle		Pistol	
	Air gun		Other					

Serial Number						
Manufacturer		Model/ Type				
Caliber		Capacity				
Weight		Identifiers				
Barrel Length		Barrel Type		Standard		Target	
				Bull		Other	

Action:	Single Shot		Semi-Auto		Bolt		Single Action	
	Revolver		Full- Auto		Lever		Double Action	
	Pump		Muzzle Loader		Other			

Description	
Alterations	
Repairs	

✎ NOTES

ACQUISITION & DISPOSITION INFORMATION

PURCHASED FROM	
ADDRESS	
CONTACT NUMBER	
DATE	PRICE PAID
ID Number	D.O.B
CONDITION	
COMMENTS	

DISPOSITION

TRANSFER/SOLD TO	
ADDRESS	
CONTACT NUMBER	
DATE	PRICE SOLD
ID Number	D.O.B
LOST/ STOLEN	CONDITION
DETAILS	

IN THE EVENT OF MY DEMISE I WANT THIS FIREARM TO GO TO:

NOTES

FIREARM DETAILS

GUN #	

FIREARM TYPE	Handgun		Shotgun		Rifle		Pistol	
	Air gun		Other					

Serial Number							
Manufacturer		Model/ Type					
Caliber		Capacity					
Weight		Identifiers					
Barrel Length		Barrel Type		Standard		Target	
				Bull		Other	
Action:	Single Shot	Semi-Auto	Bolt	Single Action	
	Revolver	Full- Auto	Lever	Double Action	
	Pump	Muzzle Loader	Other		
Description							
Alterations							
Repairs							

✎ **NOTES**

ACQUISITION & DISPOSITION INFORMATION

PURCHASED FROM	
ADDRESS	
CONTACT NUMBER	
DATE	PRICE PAID
ID Number	D.O.B
CONDITION	
COMMENTS	

DISPOSITION

TRANSFER/SOLD TO	
ADDRESS	
CONTACT NUMBER	
DATE	PRICE SOLD
ID Number	D.O.B
LOST/ STOLEN	CONDITION
DETAILS	

IN THE EVENT OF MY DEMISE I WANT THIS FIREARM TO GO TO:

NOTES

FIREARM DETAILS

GUN #

FIREARM TYPE	Handgun		Shotgun		Rifle		Pistol	
	Air gun		Other					

Serial Number				
Manufacturer		Model/ Type		
Caliber		Capacity		
Weight		Identifiers		

Barrel Length		Barrel Type	Standard	Target	
			Bull	Other	

Action:	Single Shot		Semi-Auto		Bolt		Single Action	
	Revolver		Full- Auto		Lever		Double Action	
	Pump		Muzzle Loader		Other			

Description	
Alterations	
Repairs	

✎ **NOTES**

ACQUISITION & DISPOSITION INFORMATION

PURCHASED FROM	
ADDRESS	
CONTACT NUMBER	
DATE	PRICE PAID
ID Number	D.O.B
CONDITION	
COMMENTS	

DISPOSITION

TRANSFER/SOLD TO	
ADDRESS	
CONTACT NUMBER	
DATE	PRICE SOLD
ID Number	D.O.B
LOST/ STOLEN	CONDITION
DETAILS	

IN THE EVENT OF MY DEMISE I WANT THIS FIREARM TO GO TO:	

NOTES

FIREARM DETAILS

GUN #

FIREARM TYPE	Handgun		Shotgun		Rifle		Pistol	
	Air gun		Other					

Serial Number							
Manufacturer		Model/ Type					
Caliber		Capacity					
Weight		Identifiers					
Barrel Length		Barrel Type		Standard		Target	
				Bull		Other	
Action:	Single Shot	Semi-Auto	Bolt	Single Action	
	Revolver	Full- Auto	Lever	Double Action	
	Pump	Muzzle Loader	Other		
Description							
Alterations							
Repairs							

✎ **NOTES**

ACQUISITION & DISPOSITION INFORMATION

PURCHASED FROM	
ADDRESS	
CONTACT NUMBER	
DATE	PRICE PAID
ID Number	D.O.B
CONDITION	
COMMENTS	

DISPOSITION

TRANSFER/SOLD TO	
ADDRESS	
CONTACT NUMBER	
DATE	PRICE SOLD
ID Number	D.O.B
LOST/ STOLEN	CONDITION
DETAILS	

IN THE EVENT OF MY DEMISE I WANT THIS FIREARM TO GO TO:

NOTES

FIREARM DETAILS

GUN #

FIREARM TYPE	Handgun	Shotgun	Rifle	Pistol	
	Air gun	Other			

Serial Number				
Manufacturer		Model/ Type		
Caliber		Capacity		
Weight		Identifiers		
Barrel Length		Barrel Type	Standard	Target
			Bull	Other

Action:	Single Shot	Semi-Auto	Bolt	Single Action	
	Revolver	Full- Auto	Lever	Double Action	
	Pump	Muzzle Loader	Other		

Description	
Alterations	
Repairs	

✎ **NOTES**

ACQUISITION & DISPOSITION INFORMATION

PURCHASED FROM	
ADDRESS	
CONTACT NUMBER	
DATE	PRICE PAID
ID Number	D.O.B
CONDITION	
COMMENTS	

DISPOSITION

TRANSFER/SOLD TO	
ADDRESS	
CONTACT NUMBER	
DATE	PRICE SOLD
ID Number	D.O.B
LOST/ STOLEN	CONDITION
DETAILS	

IN THE EVENT OF MY DEMISE I WANT THIS FIREARM TO GO TO:	

NOTES

_____

_____

_____

_____

_____

_____

_____

FIREARM DETAILS

GUN #

FIREARM TYPE	Handgun		Shotgun		Rifle		Pistol	
	Air gun		Other					

Serial Number								
Manufacturer		Model/ Type						
Caliber		Capacity						
Weight		Identifiers						
Barrel Length		Barrel Type		Standard		Target		
				Bull		Other		
Action:	Single Shot		Semi-Auto		Bolt		Single Action	
	Revolver		Full- Auto		Lever		Double Action	
	Pump		Muzzle Loader		Other			
Description								
Alterations								
Repairs								

✎ **NOTES**

ACQUISITION & DISPOSITION INFORMATION

PURCHASED FROM	
ADDRESS	
CONTACT NUMBER	
DATE	PRICE PAID
ID Number	D.O.B
CONDITION	
COMMENTS	

DISPOSITION

TRANSFER/SOLD TO	
ADDRESS	
CONTACT NUMBER	
DATE	PRICE SOLD
ID Number	D.O.B
LOST/ STOLEN	CONDITION
DETAILS	

IN THE EVENT OF MY DEMISE I WANT THIS FIREARM TO GO TO:

NOTES

FIREARM DETAILS

GUN #

FIREARM TYPE	Handgun	Shotgun	Rifle	Pistol	
	Air gun	Other			

Serial Number							
Manufacturer		Model/ Type					
Caliber		Capacity					
Weight		Identifiers					
Barrel Length		Barrel Type		Standard		Target	
				Bull		Other	
Action:	Single Shot	Semi-Auto	Bolt	Single Action	
	Revolver	Full- Auto	Lever	Double Action	
	Pump	Muzzle Loader	Other		
Description					
Alterations					
Repairs					

✎ NOTES

75

ACQUISITION & DISPOSITION INFORMATION

PURCHASED FROM	
ADDRESS	
CONTACT NUMBER	
DATE	PRICE PAID	
ID Number	D.O.B	
CONDITION	
COMMENTS	

DISPOSITION

TRANSFER/SOLD TO	
ADDRESS	
CONTACT NUMBER	
DATE	PRICE SOLD	
ID Number	D.O.B	
LOST/ STOLEN	CONDITION	
DETAILS	

IN THE EVENT OF MY DEMISE I WANT THIS FIREARM TO GO TO:

NOTES

FIREARM DETAILS

GUN #

FIREARM TYPE	Handgun		Shotgun		Rifle		Pistol	
	Air gun		Other					

Serial Number								
Manufacturer		Model/ Type						
Caliber		Capacity						
Weight		Identifiers						
Barrel Length		Barrel Type			Standard		Target	
					Bull		Other	
Action:	Single Shot		Semi-Auto		Bolt		Single Action	
	Revolver		Full- Auto		Lever		Double Action	
	Pump		Muzzle Loader		Other			
Description								
Alterations								
Repairs								
✎ NOTES								

ACQUISITION & DISPOSITION INFORMATION

PURCHASED FROM	
ADDRESS	
CONTACT NUMBER	
DATE	PRICE PAID
ID Number	D.O.B
CONDITION	
COMMENTS	

DISPOSITION

TRANSFER/SOLD TO	
ADDRESS	
CONTACT NUMBER	
DATE	PRICE SOLD
ID Number	D.O.B
LOST/ STOLEN	CONDITION
DETAILS	

IN THE EVENT OF MY DEMISE I WANT THIS FIREARM TO GO TO:	

NOTES

FIREARM DETAILS

GUN #	

FIREARM TYPE	Handgun		Shotgun		Rifle		Pistol	
	Air gun		Other					

Serial Number				
Manufacturer		Model/ Type		
Caliber		Capacity		
Weight		Identifiers		
Barrel Length		Barrel Type	Standard	Target
			Bull	Other

Action:	Single Shot		Semi-Auto		Bolt		Single Action	
	Revolver		Full- Auto		Lever		Double Action	
	Pump		Muzzle Loader		Other			

Description	
Alterations	
Repairs	

✎ **NOTES**

ACQUISITION & DISPOSITION INFORMATION

PURCHASED FROM	
ADDRESS	
CONTACT NUMBER	
DATE	PRICE PAID	
ID Number	D.O.B	
CONDITION	
COMMENTS	

DISPOSITION

TRANSFER/SOLD TO	
ADDRESS	
CONTACT NUMBER	
DATE	PRICE SOLD	
ID Number	D.O.B	
LOST/ STOLEN	CONDITION	
DETAILS	

IN THE EVENT OF MY DEMISE I WANT THIS FIREARM TO GO TO:

NOTES

FIREARM DETAILS

GUN #	

FIREARM TYPE	Handgun		Shotgun		Rifle		Pistol	
	Air gun		Other					

Serial Number						
Manufacturer		Model/ Type				
Caliber		Capacity				
Weight		Identifiers				
Barrel Length		Barrel Type		Standard		Target	
				Bull		Other	

Action:	Single Shot		Semi-Auto		Bolt		Single Action	
	Revolver		Full- Auto		Lever		Double Action	
	Pump		Muzzle Loader		Other			

Description	
Alterations	
Repairs	

✎ **NOTES**

ACQUISITION & DISPOSITION INFORMATION

PURCHASED FROM	
ADDRESS	
CONTACT NUMBER	
DATE		PRICE PAID	
ID Number		D.O.B	
CONDITION	
COMMENTS	

DISPOSITION

TRANSFER/SOLD TO	
ADDRESS	
CONTACT NUMBER	
DATE		PRICE SOLD	
ID Number		D.O.B	
LOST/ STOLEN		CONDITION	
DETAILS	

IN THE EVENT OF MY DEMISE I WANT THIS FIREARM TO GO TO:

NOTES

FIREARM DETAILS

GUN #

FIREARM TYPE	Handgun		Shotgun		Rifle		Pistol	
	Air gun		Other					

Serial Number				
Manufacturer		Model/ Type		
Caliber		Capacity		
Weight		Identifiers		

Barrel Length		Barrel Type	Standard	Target	
			Bull	Other	

Action:	Single Shot	Semi-Auto	Bolt	Single Action	
	Revolver	Full- Auto	Lever	Double Action	
	Pump	Muzzle Loader	Other		

Description	
Alterations	
Repairs	

✎ **NOTES**

ACQUISITION & DISPOSITION INFORMATION

PURCHASED FROM	
ADDRESS	
CONTACT NUMBER	
DATE	PRICE PAID
ID Number	D.O.B
CONDITION	
COMMENTS	

DISPOSITION

TRANSFER/SOLD TO	
ADDRESS	
CONTACT NUMBER	
DATE	PRICE SOLD
ID Number	D.O.B
LOST/ STOLEN	CONDITION
DETAILS	

IN THE EVENT OF MY DEMISE I WANT THIS FIREARM TO GO TO:	

NOTES

FIREARM DETAILS

GUN #

FIREARM TYPE	Handgun		Shotgun		Rifle		Pistol	
	Air gun		Other					

Serial Number							
Manufacturer		Model/ Type					
Caliber		Capacity					
Weight		Identifiers					
Barrel Length		Barrel Type		Standard		Target	
				Bull		Other	
Action:	Single Shot		Semi-Auto		Bolt		Single Action	
	Revolver		Full- Auto		Lever		Double Action	
	Pump		Muzzle Loader		Other			
Description							
Alterations							
Repairs							

✎ **NOTES**

ACQUISITION & DISPOSITION INFORMATION

PURCHASED FROM	
ADDRESS	
CONTACT NUMBER	
DATE		PRICE PAID	
ID Number		D.O.B	
CONDITION	
COMMENTS	

DISPOSITION

TRANSFER/SOLD TO	
ADDRESS	
CONTACT NUMBER	
DATE		PRICE SOLD	
ID Number		D.O.B	
LOST/ STOLEN		CONDITION	
DETAILS	

IN THE EVENT OF MY DEMISE I WANT THIS FIREARM TO GO TO:	

NOTES

FIREARM DETAILS

GUN #

FIREARM TYPE	Handgun		Shotgun		Rifle		Pistol	
	Air gun		Other					

Serial Number							
Manufacturer		Model/ Type					
Caliber		Capacity					
Weight		Identifiers					
Barrel Length		Barrel Type		Standard		Target	
				Bull		Other	
Action:	Single Shot	Semi-Auto	Bolt	Single Action	
	Revolver	Full- Auto	Lever	Double Action	
	Pump	Muzzle Loader	Other		
Description							
Alterations							
Repairs							

✎ NOTES

PURCHASED FROM	
ADDRESS	
CONTACT NUMBER	
DATE	PRICE PAID
ID Number	D.O.B
CONDITION	
COMMENTS	

DISPOSITION

TRANSFER/SOLD TO	
ADDRESS	
CONTACT NUMBER	
DATE	PRICE SOLD
ID Number	D.O.B
LOST/ STOLEN	CONDITION
DETAILS	

IN THE EVENT OF MY DEMISE I WANT THIS FIREARM TO GO TO:

NOTES

FIREARM DETAILS

GUN #

FIREARM TYPE	Handgun		Shotgun		Rifle		Pistol	
	Air gun		Other					

Serial Number							
Manufacturer		Model/ Type					
Caliber		Capacity					
Weight		Identifiers					
Barrel Length		Barrel Type		Standard		Target	
				Bull		Other	
Action:	Single Shot	Semi-Auto	Bolt	Single Action			
	Revolver	Full- Auto	Lever	Double Action			
	Pump	Muzzle Loader	Other				
Description							
Alterations							
Repairs							
✎ NOTES							

89

ACQUISITION & DISPOSITION INFORMATION

PURCHASED FROM	
ADDRESS	
CONTACT NUMBER	
DATE		PRICE PAID	
ID Number		D.O.B	
CONDITION	
COMMENTS	

DISPOSITION

TRANSFER/SOLD TO	
ADDRESS	
CONTACT NUMBER	
DATE		PRICE SOLD	
ID Number		D.O.B	
LOST/ STOLEN		CONDITION	
DETAILS	

IN THE EVENT OF MY DEMISE I WANT THIS FIREARM TO GO TO:	

NOTES

_____

_____

_____

_____

_____

_____

_____

FIREARM DETAILS

GUN #	

FIREARM TYPE	Handgun		Shotgun		Rifle		Pistol	
	Air gun		Other					

Serial Number	

Manufacturer		Model/ Type	
Caliber		Capacity	
Weight		Identifiers	

Barrel Length		Barrel Type		Standard		Target	
				Bull		Other	

Action:	Single Shot		Semi-Auto		Bolt		Single Action	
	Revolver		Full- Auto		Lever		Double Action	
	Pump		Muzzle Loader		Other			

Description	
Alterations	
Repairs	

✎ **NOTES**

ACQUISITION & DISPOSITION INFORMATION

PURCHASED FROM	
ADDRESS	
CONTACT NUMBER	
DATE	PRICE PAID
ID Number	D.O.B
CONDITION	
COMMENTS	

DISPOSITION

TRANSFER/SOLD TO	
ADDRESS	
CONTACT NUMBER	
DATE	PRICE SOLD
ID Number	D.O.B
LOST/ STOLEN	CONDITION
DETAILS	

IN THE EVENT OF MY DEMISE I WANT THIS FIREARM TO GO TO:

NOTES

FIREARM DETAILS

GUN #

FIREARM TYPE	Handgun		Shotgun		Rifle		Pistol	
	Air gun		Other					

Serial Number							
Manufacturer		Model/ Type					
Caliber		Capacity					
Weight		Identifiers					
Barrel Length		Barrel Type		Standard		Target	
				Bull		Other	
Action:	Single Shot	Semi-Auto	Bolt	Single Action	
	Revolver	Full- Auto	Lever	Double Action	
	Pump	Muzzle Loader	Other		
Description							
Alterations							
Repairs							

✎ **NOTES**

ACQUISITION & DISPOSITION INFORMATION

PURCHASED FROM	
ADDRESS	
CONTACT NUMBER	
DATE	PRICE PAID
ID Number	D.O.B
CONDITION	
COMMENTS	

DISPOSITION

TRANSFER/SOLD TO	
ADDRESS	
CONTACT NUMBER	
DATE	PRICE SOLD
ID Number	D.O.B
LOST/ STOLEN	CONDITION
DETAILS	

IN THE EVENT OF MY DEMISE I WANT THIS FIREARM TO GO TO:	

NOTES

FIREARM DETAILS

GUN #

FIREARM TYPE	Handgun		Shotgun		Rifle		Pistol	
	Air gun		Other					

Serial Number				
Manufacturer		Model/ Type		
Caliber		Capacity		
Weight		Identifiers		

Barrel Length		Barrel Type	Standard		Target	
			Bull		Other	

Action:	Single Shot	Semi-Auto	Bolt	Single Action	
	Revolver	Full- Auto	Lever	Double Action	
	Pump	Muzzle Loader	Other		

Description	
Alterations	
Repairs	

✎ **NOTES**

ACQUISITION & DISPOSITION INFORMATION

PURCHASED FROM	
ADDRESS	
CONTACT NUMBER	
DATE	PRICE PAID
ID Number	D.O.B
CONDITION	
COMMENTS	

DISPOSITION

TRANSFER/SOLD TO	
ADDRESS	
CONTACT NUMBER	
DATE	PRICE SOLD
ID Number	D.O.B
LOST/ STOLEN	CONDITION
DETAILS	

IN THE EVENT OF MY DEMISE I WANT THIS FIREARM TO GO TO:	

NOTES

FIREARM DETAILS

GUN #

FIREARM TYPE	Handgun		Shotgun		Rifle		Pistol	
	Air gun		Other					

Serial Number								
Manufacturer		Model/ Type						
Caliber		Capacity						
Weight		Identifiers						
Barrel Length		Barrel Type		Standard		Target		
				Bull		Other		
Action:	Single Shot	Semi-Auto		Bolt		Single Action		
	Revolver	Full- Auto		Lever		Double Action		
	Pump	Muzzle Loader		Other				
Description								
Alterations								
Repairs								
✎ NOTES								

ACQUISITION & DISPOSITION INFORMATION

PURCHASED FROM	
ADDRESS	
CONTACT NUMBER	
DATE	PRICE PAID
ID Number	D.O.B
CONDITION	
COMMENTS	

DISPOSITION

TRANSFER/SOLD TO	
ADDRESS	
CONTACT NUMBER	
DATE	PRICE SOLD
ID Number	D.O.B
LOST/ STOLEN	CONDITION
DETAILS	

IN THE EVENT OF MY DEMISE I WANT THIS FIREARM TO GO TO:

NOTES

FIREARM DETAILS

GUN #

FIREARM TYPE	Handgun		Shotgun		Rifle		Pistol	
	Air gun		Other					

Serial Number							
Manufacturer			Model/ Type				
Caliber			Capacity				
Weight			Identifiers				
Barrel Length			Barrel Type		Standard		Target	
					Bull		Other	

Action:	Single Shot		Semi-Auto		Bolt		Single Action	
	Revolver		Full- Auto		Lever		Double Action	
	Pump		Muzzle Loader		Other			

Description	
Alterations	
Repairs	

✎ **NOTES**

ACQUISITION & DISPOSITION INFORMATION

PURCHASED FROM	
ADDRESS	
CONTACT NUMBER	
DATE	PRICE PAID
ID Number	D.O.B
CONDITION	
COMMENTS	

DISPOSITION

TRANSFER/SOLD TO	
ADDRESS	
CONTACT NUMBER	
DATE	PRICE SOLD
ID Number	D.O.B
LOST/ STOLEN	CONDITION
DETAILS	

IN THE EVENT OF MY DEMISE I WANT THIS FIREARM TO GO TO:

NOTES

_____

_____

_____

_____

_____

_____

_____

LEGAL BIT

27 CFR 478.125A - PERSONAL FIREARMS COLLECTION.

§ 478.125a Personal firearms **collection.**

(a) Notwithstanding any other provision of this subpart, a **licensed manufacturer**, **licensed importer**, or **licensed dealer** is not required to comply with the provisions of **§ 478.102** or record on a **firearms** transaction record, Form 4473, the sale or other disposition of a **firearm** maintained as part of the licensee's personal **firearms** collection: *Provided,* That

    (1) The licensee has maintained the **firearm** as part of such collection for 1 year from the date the **firearm** was transferred from the business inventory into the personal collection or otherwise acquired as a personal **firearm**,

    (2) The licensee recorded in the bound record prescribed by **§ 478.125(e)** the receipt of the **firearm** into the business inventory or other acquisition,

    (3) The licensee recorded the **firearm** as a disposition in the bound record prescribed by **§ 478.125(e)**when the **firearm** was transferred from the business inventory into the personal **firearms** collection or otherwise acquired as a personal **firearm**, and

    (4) The licensee enters the sale or other disposition of the **firearm** from the personal **firearms** collection into a bound record, under the format prescribed below, identifying the **firearm** transferred by recording the name of the **manufacturer** and **importer** (if any), the model, serial number, type, and the caliber or gauge, and showing the date of the sale or other disposition, the name and address of the transferee, or the name and business address of the transferee if such **person** is a licensee, and the date of birth of the transferee if other than a licensee. In addition, the licensee shall cause the transferee, if other than a licensee, to be identified in any manner customarily used in commercial transactions (e.g., a drivers license). The format required for the disposition record of personal **firearms** is as follows:

DISPOSITION RECORD OF PERSONAL FIREARMS

Description of firearm					Disposition		
Manufacturer and importer (if any)	Model	Serial No.	Type	Caliber or gauge	Date	Name and address (business address if licensee)	Date of birth if non licensee

(b) Any **licensed manufacturer**, **licensed importer**, or **licensed dealer** selling or otherwise disposing of a **firearm** from the licensee's personal **firearms** collection under this section shall be subject to the restrictions imposed by the **Act** and this part on the dispositions of **firearms** by **persons** other than licensed manufacturers, licensed importers, and licensed dealers.

Made in the USA
Middletown, DE
29 May 2019